Reverie's Ilk: Collected Prose Poems

Karl Elder

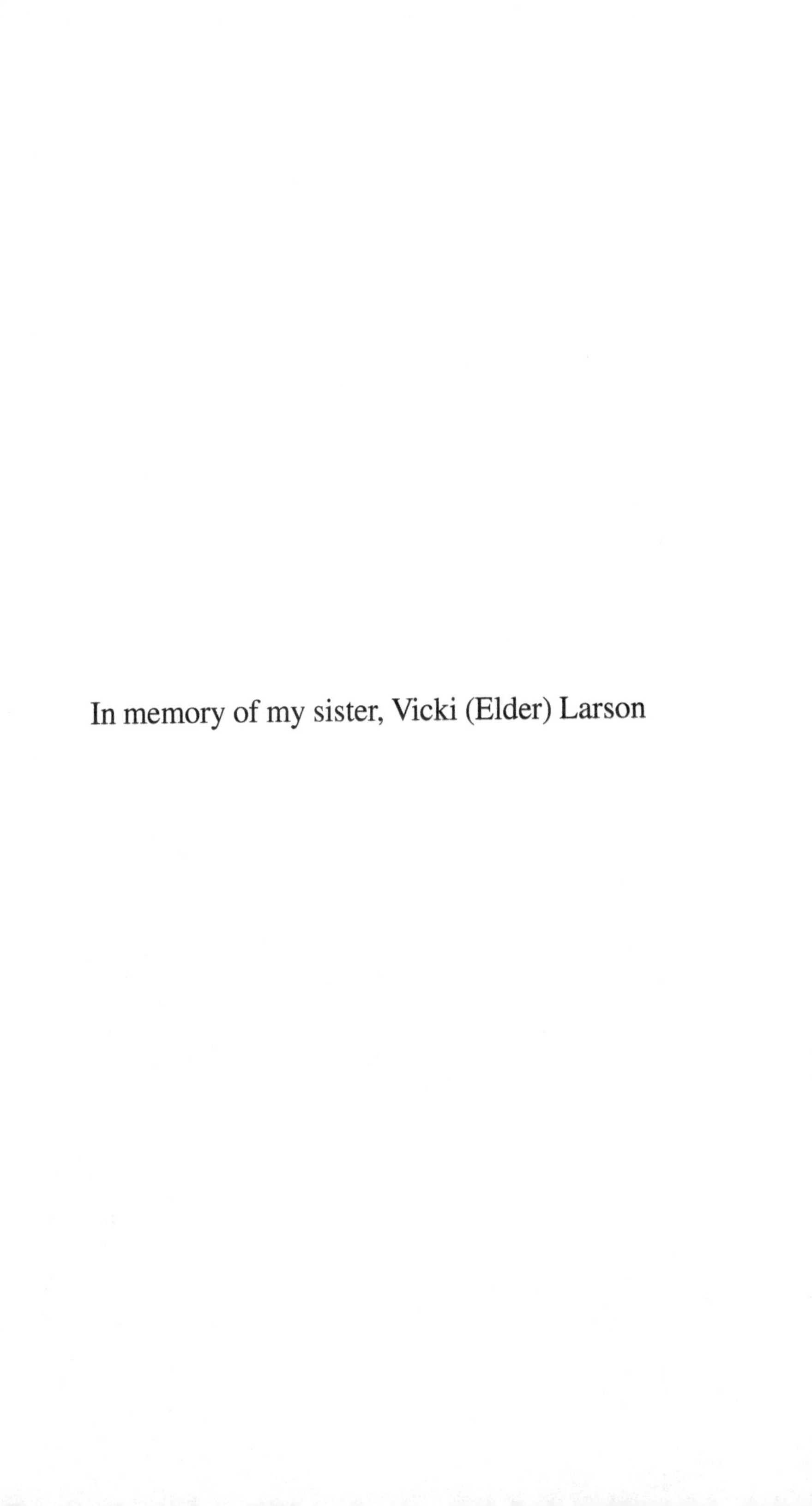

In memory of my sister, Vicki (Elder) Larson

My enduring gratitude to the editors of the following magazines and anthologies in which, over a span of five decades, one or more pieces comprising *Reverie's Ilk* have appeared:

580 Split, *Ascent*, *Birmingham Poetry Review*, *Cthulhu Haiku and Other Mythos Madness*, *Dacotah Territory*, *Edgz*, *Elm*, *Free Verse*, *Halloween Haiku*, *High Plains Literary Review*, *Madrona*, *Making It Speak: Poets and Artists in Cahoots*, *Mangrove*, *Pacific Review*, *Phantasm*, *The Plastic Tower*, *The Prose Poem*, *The Prosery*, *qarrtsiluni*, *Slipstream*, *Stoneboat*, *riverSedge*, *Runes*, *Standing Wave*, *Transactions*, *Winewood Journal*, *Wisconsin Review*, and *Verse Wisconsin*.

Contents

Learning to Talk 7

A Life 8

The Cockroach 9

Prepubescence 10

While She Is Away 11

Sentiment 12

Jade Plant 13

A Dead Thing 14

As Hunger Does Sometimes Dial Long Distance 15

Bluegills 16

To L. N. in Heaven 17

An August 18

Fast Approaching Forty 19

Within the Book and Volume of My Brain 20

The Ghoul 21

The Elders 22

The Spell 25

The Rock 26

The Great American Novel 27

Dream: Accountability 28

Schizophrenia 29

These Dank Woods 30

They Hauled a Hunk of the Moon 31

A Halo of Gnats 32

Dream: Killer Babies 33

Skull 34

Ye Shall Brush Your Teeth 35

Dream in Five Acts 36

Dream: The Intangible 38

Recreations 39

Revelation 42

The World Is Ugly and the People Are Sad 43

The Finger 44

There Was Nobody Famous 45

The They in "What will they think of next?" 46

Where Silence Rains..47

Faith 48

Miracle 49

The Black Brick 50

Cold Feet..51

The Tailgater 52

The Betrayal 53

The Loaves and the Fishes 54

Two Religions 55

Testaments 56

The Sentence 59

Learning to Talk

There is another organ beside the tongue that does not scar. The brain. It is there among convolutions you had your most fluent dream of the bean you snuffed up a nostril at four where it took root.

Is it any wonder you stole the bean from your mother's pantry? Is there any doubt it is why on occasion, like a blind man, you think with your hand? Your fingers, they are tunnels for you to travel to depths you have not known but felt when, as a child, you'd be on your belly, burrowing with your entire arm beneath damp sand you'd made a mountain of.

Likewise there are mountains and caves you have made in the mind, airy vowels and dark consonants, as if language were made of words and not the urge they represent to go on talking, this inexplicable surge of energy from atoms and quarks that arrange themselves, here, instead of on some distant star, instead of where you are.

A Life

With both hands a small boy holds a ball of string so big it doesn't occur to him there are two ends, so far from him is the center. It is only after the string is tied to the kite, the ball growing smaller—yet, with each glance, more vivid—that he can predict a beginning, the nothing the sphere is wound around.

So it is that somewhere between boy and man he is made to understand that the atom, too, is hollow, and therefore the universe. He comes to see that this is how his life will go, that the string unwinding so fast, which at the very last he was unable to hold, had nothing to do with a beginning or an end, but—like the makings of the sphere—everything to do with both.

The Cockroach

Not tall enough to use the urinal in Union Station, my youngest settles on the third stall he inspects, relatively clean, until something he's not seen in his life chases him out, a cockroach to rival any I've met, mean as a mongoose I remember saying once in the Far East, so that Wade's shout won't scare him off, though shrill enough to stifle the snores behind the door of the next stall over. Later, of course, there are questions. Like why don't they mop the vomit. And why was that man sleeping in there. So I tell him.

And now a week later I want to take it back. Not that I lied. Or even told the truth. But as I watch him boldly swim for the first time just beneath the surface, as if to defy the net, his even bluer eyes open underwater, searching for my hands, and as I lift him slick, sputtering, wide-eyed, and for the moment bald, I look into his face, that Tweety Bird face absent its coyness.

Wade, what we saw that time on vacation when we got off the train. I wish it were not real-life. Just somebody's art with a capital "A." But that's not what I mean. What's important is I stamped my foot. The cockroach vanished. You, you went in there and you went. And that man. Why—when we didn't see so much as his face—did I make him out so low as to have a cockroach for a pet, as if a man who swims could not possibly drown. Let this be a lesson. I was the one not afraid, who now am.

Prepubescence

He was six when in the office he colored this big black keyhole on a blue Post-It and stuck it to the edge of a shelf. It's like a cartoon door on a dungeon without walls or windows. Sometimes I've moved it, unconsciously, hunting a book, yet a hundred times stood before a thing so stark it seemed there before he made it, what only a child could see to create, a reminder he can't be reminded of it, that for now there's no escape.

While She Is Away

The pipe is a sculptured meerschaum, and just as I sense she's about to ask, "What tobacco is that?" meaning "I like your cologne," I wield it from my teeth, yet balance it so quietly on the table that the bowl grows an endless strand of blue hair, so swiftly carried to the far side of perception, so very beautifully, I somehow know why love is a word I no longer need, and while my eye is fixed, she eases alongside me, slips my wrist and hand on like some elegant ornament, and places it, palm up, in my lap.

Sentiment

How *can* this be? Here I am, driving to Baskin-Robbins six months later, and for no reason I begin weeping uncontrollably for my molars—those crude, excavated pairs of dice whose numbers had finally come up. Their absence creates a real scene—my tongue darting from one hollow to the other, a new mother in search of her pups. "O Fate!" she cries, translating inhibition, rendering the loss in an image I can understand: stunted, bloody rooks toppled on the dentist's table as he shifts strategy, playing with himself on the hinged game board of my jaws. I stop the car. I shove it in reverse, determined to take a correspondence course, anything to gain knowledge of their where-abouts, the wisdom of another profession.

Jade Plant

She's calling me a *dumb* fart and yelling why didn't I unload the dishwasher and look at this shit smeared everywhere like the peanut butter on the counter as if this place were a goddamned sandwich or something, and I jump up and stomp over at her jade plant for reasons unbeknownst to me and bend over and go blah! blah! blah-blah! and it just sits there, green with envy, hundreds of fat, dumb tongues.

A Dead Thing

When on these mornings there's no money to be made, we walk, long walks, a marriage taking time and memory, time to remember to forget about money. Sometimes we talk and maybe this time—I forget—but as we stride along the outside of a big curve, there's a dead thing coming up on our side of the road and I resolve I won't look at it or speak of it on our approach.

"What is it?" she says, and I say "opossum," my tongue stumbling, though the mind knows the o is silent.

"*Aw, Boy* (her word for *Honey*), it isn't dead yet! What'll we *do?*"

So I slow and backtrack a bit, and there it is, a giant rat wrapped in gray fur, curled like a big shrimp but with a tail like something a kid rolled from clay and an impossible grin on a snout that barely revolves with the neck, movement motorized, as if a figure in the mall's Christmas scene.

"Kill it," I answer, quiet.

"I *couldn't* kill it," she blurts. "The poor thing. Oh," she says, "this is making me sick!"

We walk on. We don't talk. And I, a mile away, hear myself say under my breath, "What with?"

I study her hands.

I look at mine.

I have not known such poverty.

Such wealth.

As Hunger Does Sometimes Dial Long Distance

Thought at first my stomach growled, as hunger does sometimes dial long distance, which is you calling yourself, ring off, that purr in your ear, until its guttural bubbled into a whole note that softly broke in something simmering over my shoulder: sweet silence released from some sauce here in her kitchen: the future, which has shrunk to this: a meal had of the moment.

Bluegills

Were I to become a widower, I'd fish bluegills. The calm of early morning water'd remind me of this moment beside the sleeping Brenda. Her mind teems with a story told in the movement of her foot as much as her typing fingers—this spasm, that flutter felt in the taut line.

That's what's perfect about bluegills. The quick yet repeated mystery: not the catch nor its splash, but before, now, and always, the fish dumbly mouthing its hunger as if the story must be told through the dream of this woman—the story, I want to tell her, of my own.

To L. N. in Heaven

As the eye cannot see the mite that inhabits it, so are men blind to contagion. This you knew twenty years ago without me telling you—Ft. Lewis, Ord, or on Okinawa. What I now must tell myself is why, without a war going on, you died. For love? Now, you tell me, what do you think of the life that killed you? You in Portland hiding behind a hospice phone in skin and bones I only let myself imagine. When your friend called with your last goodbye, news of the end of your suffering, I could not think to ask what he meant to you. I dwell as I have these five years, whenever I see the acronym, on the inscrutability of it, stupidly wondering at your horror of maybe having passed it on (there was always that we dared not speak, though at least I know what could not be known). You said you thought it would not have mattered you were gay, which meant, of course, there was the chance it would. There remains, after all, that war they had us psyched to fight. How I wept at your confession and again this April under cherry blossoms, having sensed your ghost as I walked, unable to look, along the polished wall, learning what we might have had and, only at your passing, have.

An August

You water coneflowers at the edge of the wild island on your lawn to turn, to see without warning another one has sprung in its season out of season, a mushroom. To weed but one seems a waste so you wander in a pattern random as seed flung by the wind, bend, pick, until your hand holds a whole harvest of soft rocks, which you pitch to the island.

Is this what it has come to? Your wife's rage for order now spreading to the lawn like yellow across a page in a book too long in the sun? Or are you here because you've gone underground, a man standing on an expanse of asphalt and lawns, smelling his damp hands. Wasn't it last night on this very lawn you awoke to the stars, standing, wondering was this the dream you had when twenty years ago you wished under some of these same stars there would be time to stare at stars? Is this why we have lawns. To have stars? No, you were not then an Elizabeth. Nor were you seven. You were twenty-seven, though you do not know now how.

Always there was August. Never were there mushrooms in August. They are like the stars; they are constellations that come out at night. They are the flavor of wet newspaper and their light, like the light of stars, is old news. This is how to look at the stars is to go underground. This is how to greet the grave.

You must greet the grave still alive. You must say never will there be another August like this. A lawn this lush. For there has been the right rain and its karma, fog. For what is fog but rain refined? And what is rain but another thing you cup you can't hold in your hands? Were someone to come along to see you linger here, head bowed and fingers woven, they might think you are praying. Not looking at your life.

Fast Approaching Forty

Even in perceptively evaporating light, even as he beats these weeds for a baseball while friends wait for him to show with the poker chips, he is actually happy. How exact the thing is lost till the instant it's found, he remembers, still searching. Parting a giant thistle with his brand new glove, the only he's owned since Lord knows where he lost or who lifted the first, twenty-five years ago, despite his name burned on back with a magnifying glass—the pristine patience it took of a June morning, like one long summer as sweet as the clover blossom he'd pluck from behind the backstop to suck in the outfield—he knows without thought the distance between him and his death is infinitely divisible, having put it all behind him, his very birth someone else's version of yet another's suffering.

Yet time will not be the talk at the poker table. He will speak of box scores and things, that in a game called pass the shit, you never refuse an ace. He will not talk about the lost ball either, assuming even, fast approaching forty, he finds it. And certainly he will not talk about a receipt for the ball and gloves, how as it slipped from his fingers when he got out of the car and as it zig-zagged leaf-like to the concrete, he stopped to watch, yet did not stoop to where it lay, and still lies, but stood to marvel how, even while playing father to his sons, detachment to moments of his own making remains so massive, so finally incomplete.

Within the Book and Volume of My Brain

1.   I said to the living, "Well, when *I* go, do with me what you will." But what I secretly want is something like a soft monument where someone could lay his head and read, what I imagine you finally want, as lonely now as the living.

2.   What I can't stand, I told Brenda one night after a fight over just about everything, is I'll never see you again.

3.   Although I see you often. See you sitting in bed as I slipped out of your room for the last time, see your expression, your father's face I saw in both coffins.

The shade of the maple over you is shaded by the Earth to which I cling these nights like a dark moth on black bark.

We revolve. Even the dead. We turn on the face of the Earth. Even the living lying in their beds on their backs, awake.

The Ghoul

Instead of on to the junction—a word you'd magically tie to some rhyme, as though there was a story behind it, when I was a kid and you were Dad on his route—I impulsively turn this summer night onto a street alongside a cemetery half a block wide, two blocks deep, and two hundred miles from your grave.

There is something I don't recognize until I think of it as a cloud spun behind a truck on a gravel road at sunset maybe, so thick that while in a field waiting for the farmer to finish his round you look over your shoulder from velvet weed you've pulled and you don't see dust but something like hedge for fifty yards, all the more beautiful *here* because it's ugly, obscuring the stones, the graves themselves.

Then the hedge disappears. The green begins. The stones begin.

What I love is the angles in the periphery of my headlights, the anarchy of the old chalk-like markers in stark contrast with their animated shadows as I pass. Later, driving by from the other way, I know I have a beautiful thing to keep. It will be of this grief. The title came to me first, as they sometimes do when it, the piece, feels as right as one of your stories felt even after magic became illusion, even now as this thing, this new life and acceptance, requires for its sustenance your death.

The Elders

for Vicki and Dave

I.

This is our mother and father. They are not smiling, gazing here into the future. It is 1946. They cannot know they will have much to be happy about so they wear gray suits—she with a hat, with its hint of a veil and a corsage, he with a tie. Though he stares directly at us, his shoulder is turned toward her as if she holds his left hand in her lap, which we are not allowed to see. She, she is turned slightly to the southwest if behind them is due north. It is their wedding picture. You can tell there is affection between them but not for the world. She is thirty-three and he is forty. Each has been disappointed by love.

II.

Here is a full-length shot of Karl, our mother's father, slightly stooped, his fists jammed into his pants pockets to hold the tremors to a minimum. The sun is in his face, though he grins in our grandmother's flower garden through which he shuffles as if to ward off the Parkinson's. No one would know he's over six feet. Big ears and a protruding lower lip, he knows something we do not. Always. He chews White Owls and you cannot beat him at checkers. We will see him later in the basement of the First Methodist Church in Pittsfield, Illinois standing behind a 50th wedding anniversary cake. He will be without open collar. Alta, whom he will not have been allowed to touch for the middle third of their marriage, will have dressed him. They will have, however, learned to love each other despite their anger. For the meantime he looks her right in the eye. He knows something, all right. He's always had her number. When we are kids we wear his cigar bands as though they are the insignia distinguishing us as agents of some mysterious order.   In this overly exposed snapshot he wears his white hair. As one who knows, he *is* the White Owl. He will pass away with dignity, peacefully, in his sleep. His wife will be at his side.

III.

Now here we have Alta at seventy-five, still radiant, a studio portrait, of whom her son-in-law, our father, once said, "She's a high flying babe who never landed." You know by her smile she buys big presents but would wrestle a bum for a quarter. You can hear the choir from three blocks away when she's in town on a Sunday morning. She sang opera as a girl out of St. Louis when Karl, the grocer, snagged her off the tour. Therefore her God is song and entire congregations of Methodists have heard—if not seen—God. They think she is wonderful and so do we though they cannot possibly know the extent of our awe. When she came to live with us, a trial separation from her husband, she came to cook and clean. The house became the flower garden she left behind, the store, and the restaurant. How could our mother, with her father's temperament, match her? Our mother would listen. And listen. And listen. Her mother was her mother.

IV.

Meet Amos in a rare pose without Grace, taken perhaps in the basement of the same First Methodist Church to which Karl and Alta belonged. Amos owned the other business in town—Moorman's— having moved there off the farm for a better way of life in which there was time for the Bible, Zane Gray, his fellow Masons, and his wife, whom he would attend with the enthusiasm of a cabin boy and call "Kid" even into their eighties and who herself remained active in Eastern

Star. He has the stern look of a man who will go far, having from so far away come, the deep lines in his face the mark of one destined for study, contemplation, and wisdom, while by day he tills a huge garden, makes wood, feeds the stove, and runs his bird dogs. He has the visage of a man who on the wall of his den there is an elephant gun. And there is.

V.

One needs not know her name to see the resemblance—this daughter of Providence. With an innocence that caused her to gasp in the midst of her "story," her soap opera, how she bore five children was a wonder. And that blond-red pair of halos wound and pinned above her head each morning, waist-length braids that once—visiting her house on a weekend, ready for bed—we got to unravel, help her brush twice one hundred. Absent from the portrait is her chair. Gone too to cedar chests are the elaborate doilies, the shawls, the sprawling white tablecloths she crocheted on her lap where she would lay the needles down in order to reach, to hold each face as we leaned, in turn, for a kiss. "How you wuz?" she would greet us, that playful chuckle as much an exclamation of how we had grown as it was a test of English. Grace, who as a young farm wife had an accident, who the last time she drove a car was her first, who "busted the barn door to boards," winked Amos, whose mutual love of language would have her, she of the faint heart, out of breath, as if he knew her soft laughter were her calisthenics. Now, three decades after her death, as if leaning into a Degas, a memory comes to surface. As circumstance would have it in that small house, a grandson burst in upon her dressing before her mirror, nude. I tell *you* the way she did not flinch was pure Grace.

The Spell

Finally, I drop to the sidewalk the stone I've held for a quarter hour or more, leaning at the edge of the Pigeon River bridge where at an angle below, maybe the distance from mound to home plate, a Great Blue Heron stands on the spill, a rock-and-driftwood dam, thanks to the abandoned labor of children. What luck I wear a T-shirt the shade of the heron's back! Or is it hunger that here trumps fear, as now, impossibly swift on her tucked neck, the pointed beak pivots east, toward a sun-blocked bank. Another minute. The neck uncoils into a backward question mark. Later, a dove explodes with a whistle from the brush to land in the rushes not six feet behind her head, and had I the heron's eye, I'd swear she did not blink. Then out of nowhere a second dove lands on higher ground, dump loads of rock white as chalk on the west bank. Even in midst of more flurry, even after the span it takes for the pair to mate, the question mark stays cocked. And that pose—such a taut yet specious emblem for curiosity, I think, caught as the heron is outside the net of human apprehension woven with a predilection for, say, film over a still photo, action over inaction, though with an inert point of view. As to her spell, it's no less in its lesson than the suspense: Before, at last, she vanished, banking behind cottonwood at the blunt-end bend in the river; before, quiet as a butterfly's glide, she flew low the length of the shaded corridor; before she rose, dangling legs trailing toes; before she embraced, hugely, the air in a flash of slowly expanding though sudden blue, there came at agonizing intervals the slightest, the entirely imperceptible extension of neck and attitude of bill until—quick as the spark in a patiently-wrought, dark haiku—the shot, the kill.

The Rock

This is a story of a man striking an unexpected rock in a garden he has worked for years, whether the garden is real or not. For a second he wants to look up to see his house is there, that he hasn't been plowing the neighbor's plot by mistake, but, certain this is no dream, he squats to extract the rock.

It won't budge. He shoves at it with his boot, but it won't be moved. He selects a lever and a concrete block from the shed. No matter how deep he probes there is more of the boulder.

Much later from a distance the gardener is seen with another man. They talk and gesture toward the ground. Each wears a straw hat. Both are leaning on shovels. Small mounds of clay contrast with the expanse of rich soil at their feet.

The next day the scene is so far away that the exhaust fumes from the backhoe are barely visible. There are more men now, standing in a great circle, staring down from the edge of the hole.

Nightfall. Everything is quiet. The yellow light from an aluminum awning upstairs cast on the green lawn like a single buttress remains on for an inordinately long time. At dawn a bulldozer arrives, fills the hole.

Again the scene is a close-up, the man is plowing around the rock that is the tip of an iceberg, the peak of an underground mountain, or the Earth itself—whatever. Only one thing is certain to the man: the rock is not of this world.

The Great American Novel

So a woman appears at your door in the rain. If only her hair were not limp and dripping. If only she would not shiver, as if standing, knees slightly bent, at the edge of some precipice, as if cradling her breasts as if cradling a baby. You might place her.

Instead you mistake her for your mother before you were born. The young woman is delivering a package and something that reminds you of ink is running in rivulets down her front.

By the time you earn the courage to invite her in, she is no longer nude, adorned in the manner you would be clothed were you to undress to reveal your veins, which look like blue roots, the circuitry under the suit, at times you break out in.

Now, what you thought was ink is ink. It is the story of your life. Having finally found a pen to sign for the package, all the pages within are blank. There is little left for her to do but hold you.

Dream: Accountability

This broad humping me has the same, glowing Cheshire eyes as in the Sci-Fi flick last night. She calls herself William Matthews and pulls from the crevice of a sloppy cesarean an I.D. and all the poems she has written for me. I can't believe it; they're Xeroxed from magazines. I wring my hands, which, during moments such as these, yearn for their notebook and pen. She stills them by rocking them asleep, tucking them between the warm pillows of her cleavage, whispering for them not to despair, that Xeroxing and cloning are hardly analogous. Of course, she's on top, and I am outmanned by the sheer authority of her desire.

In feigned disinterest I roll the back of my square head from one side to the other on the linoleum—a clever psychology in want of another object to stare at. We are surrounded by pointed cowboy boots filled with members of the Kansas Conference for Teachers of English Composition, who sip sherry and generally ignore us. I am beside myself. I recall a paper by one of my best students about the church converted to a massage parlor here in Wichita. It's being run off and distributed among these people without my permission. Harley Elliott has illustrated it—spots on stained glass. Now I know I'll never get a job. I begin whimpering; the rhythm of this gal in incredible. She leans into it with great satisfaction, clit like a razor, and collapses, smothering me with the fine down of her jubilant breasts, sighing in my ear she'd do just about anything to get an "A."

Schizophrenia

She had a dream she sawed off her hands. Had they, the hands, complicity? Even when she is left-handed, she cannot remember which went first or whether the dream revealed such, as though now, not her, but the hands dreamed it. Neither does she remember the utter absence of blood and how the hands clung to her wrists, wanting to be held.

It is the same way her head begs to be held when she awakens from these dreams, as if it were a China doll's head barely glued on, and like the jagged line circumscribing the neck, hairline cracks sprint around the wrists.

Likewise nowadays there are only dreams to talk about. One by one her children are leaving as though by suicide, the eldest and the baby gone—one to L.A., maybe, the other voluntarily with their father. When she fucks a man now, it's anyone but him: The man upstairs; the woman across the hall.

Each morning is a new mask for an old disguise, putting on her face. Today's wears blue eyeshadow below one lid, has perfume for her breath. Always, before she can finish, there's the cleaning woman's knock.

Once the floor is scrubbed, the place dusted, following the following-herself-around like a bitch chasing its tail, when the lavatory gleams to their mutual satisfaction, the maid explodes, quits, but not before being let go, not before the woman of the house again tenders her own resignation.

Let *them* cook supper, she thinks, the little bastards. Let them own a taste of pain. "To be or not" is not the question when there is hunger. And even if she is fed up, it doesn't mean *she* isn't hungry, hungry not for love, but what comes after—that the sensation of washing herself, say, be not touch of an other.

These Dank Woods

This morning these dank woods smell like every kind of animal urine. Atmospheres here can be so local they go subatomic, a single leaf may quake. The scratches on your shin are the same color of droplets in the raspberry patch. A kingfisher lights near a cow plop and the sandhill crane quietly glides all day in the space of a few seconds. A mile west a circle of carnies outnumbers their women two to one over doughnuts and cigarettes. A plump adolescent blond squeezes a pimple behind a trailer, staring right through her observer. Though in another place, another time, she may be the first to speak, she has slept hard, you can just tell these things, with the stuffed animals in the wagon.

They Hauled a Hunk of the Moon

They hauled a hunk of the moon back and under the cloak of daylight turned it over, gratis, to the world's greatest sculptor, known only to those in the know. His studio is in our neighborhood and what he sculpts of it is the moon in its every detail from photographs taken there. It must look like one of those big, old globes in libraries, there in the artist's back yard. Scientists come and go all night. First there is laughter. Then great wailing and the glow over the high walls of the fence.

A Halo of Gnats

Cartoon characters do not attend church but are most often observed in the holiest of places, the forest.

There we marvel at how naughty Tweety can be yet get away with it, the moms and dads of our heroes rarely around to lay down the kibosh on innocents whom we sense would rather kill than be killed, the kind of morality that allows reason to cut in line ahead of sacrifice.

But sacrifice they must—blown to kingdom come, run over over and over, or swallowed by the cat—so that when the child reaches the age of majority and goes to college he or she intuitively understands karma.

Still, these characters murder one another. How wise their maker not to paint them human and, in doing so, render them all the more— tragic souls with comic voices, tongue-tied and articulate.

Dream: Killer Babies

I am their executioner. I wear a diving mask instead of a hood, which affords me the clearest possible view of the effects of my work. I handle them with the same lack of remorse they show their victims. Their heads wobble and flop at my insistence like that of a rubber doll, their visible cries rising to the surface at the edge of the pool, where stands my witness, the man who puts meat in the mouths of my children.

Skull

While the skull reminded some of death, he was reminded of the moon, which was white and blind that October night.

Halloween was around the corner. He had three wishes. One was the skull was as alive as the moon to whom he could talk because then he could hold the moon. Two was he wanted to walk around with the moon in his hand. Three was he could not pee with the moon looking at him.

So he buried the skull in his head. Buried it dead.

Ye Shall Brush Your Teeth

Ye shall brush your teeth. Ye shall not soon bequeath. Yeah, ye shall drive your car but not so far as to be longer than far. Time will be there to greet you, time with its toothbrush in one hand and Yorick's skull in the other. You are going to a party where time is the host. You shall carry a time piece because that's the smart thing to take to time's house. Little can you know, however—though this fortune you have bought, and for which you shall want your money back, may provide you with an inkling—just how austere, how fickle, time can be with his sickle stored behind the front door or the other scythe leaning in the kitchen on the way out back. You shall be drawn to the butcher's block where there is beer. Tipsy, after a while, you shall not fear. In time you shall awake from your dream. It is the dream in which you are nosy. And because it is your nature to make the best of out of any awkward situation, you shall peek in time's freezer to discover it filled with ice cream from a regional dairy in the heart of Wisconsin, Death by Chocolate.

Dream in Five Acts

In a bar the bartender claims is frequented by Clint Eastwood I am in the army on a weekend pass in my civies. It's dark in here, really dark, it's 2 p.m., and I have been walking for hours in the California sun without something like the sunglasses I now have on and because as I sip straight gin no matter where I swivel nor how I turn I can't see behind.

"This is one dark bar room," I say, pointing at the mirror. I say, "Where does he sit?"

The bartender says, "What?"

"Eastwood," I say, "where does he sit?"

"He sits where you're sitting, only he's taller."

The way the bartender says *taller* I know it is the end of act one.

Act two is the same scene only the bartender is a woman, and taller. Because I am in the army I've never seen a woman in my life and I am taller. It is a good thing I have sunglasses on. I cannot believe I am married and I am not here with her, my wife, that is, not the bartender. When we were on vacation in San Francisco a year ago I was with her, my wife, that is, not the bartender. Here I am in the army in Monterey where a glance is a stare. It must be the atmosphere, spare, cavernous, in fact, where you are served gin over diamonds you can crunch and they disappear.

"I hear Clint Eastwood frequents here," I tell her.

I'm in the army and it's act three, California, a cave in the city of Monterey.

"You could be him," she says, "for all I know. The guy wears a disguise."

In comes another customer looking like Abraham Lincoln, who orders an Olympia and walks it up the far end of the bar and thus toward my chair. I'm in the army and I'm not surprised he knows, though lately in different mirrors I never look the same way twice.

I tell him so in the fourth act. It is my affliction, I say. Abe is so honest, so innocent, I think he believes me as my fists fence each other with little plastic swords that held plump, stuffed olives, reminding me of eyes that never blink.

"No, really," I wink, "I'm in Monterey in a cave because I shaved off my mustache in the army up the road at Ord because my C.O. made me. I'm married so don't try to hit on me and that goes for you too, Missy."

Abe orders me an Olympia.

By act five, arms draped over each other's shoulders, Abe is calling me Clint. I've got a makeup artist so good I wear a Karl Elder suit. Abe's ears and beard are both on the bar, and absent the get-up he looks a lot like the guy in the mirror. It is February, 1972, and I'm writing a Valentine to my wife in Illinois on a cocktail napkin in a cave the bartender on an earlier shift claims is frequented by me, Clint Eastwood, who is in the army on a weekend pass. It's dark in here and Abe Lincoln who looks more like me every minute is my understudy in a dream about Monterey and wants to know the secret of life.

"Kid," I say, "you're barking up the wrong tree."

Dream: The Intangible

Jon Stangel leads me on a walk buckling with rungs of grass to a garage of gray, vertical slats. He's about to embark on a new career. Do I remember that thing he became involved with? Others gather as he demonstrates the product, the name for which is unforgettable. Hearing it, as if by magic I'm able to predict what is behind the double doors, that now swing open, revealing two units hung on either door by the plastic straps on their handles. It's a combination freezer\vacuum. Suddenly I must own this machine simply because he can let it go at a sacrifice for a thousand. I remember that weeks before he bought one for a hundred. He is paper rich, although not too rich, since there are but five in the world. He shows us how, as an added feature, the thing will tune a car, which only serves to whet my desire. I know on the spot I will withdraw my life's savings, fated to make huge returns on my investment. I beat it for the bank.

When I return I get a closer look. The view I have is a profile: it's chrome and white, the exaggerated features of an electric broom, a tiny door in the back, except there's no compartment or even a Small bag to collect crumbs. Now I see it is art and therefore the finest imaginable investment. I'm so excited that the thousand dollar bill begins to smolder in my hand, then flame. I say, Here, quick, take it, but Jon seems reluctant. I look into his sad eyes. Too bad, they say, you could have known wealth beyond your wildest dreams. I transfer the money to my left hand, violently shaking it, but it flames there too. The more I snap my wrist, the more air the fire is fed until *poof*, the bill is gone.

Recreations

Life

and god said let there be light and in his arm waving exuberance
knocked the whole damned box of kitchen matches off the stove
tumbling through the trap door which erupted into millions of matches
falling through the great shaft toward Earth attached here on the wall
of the universe where the box already lay since naturally it was heavier
and the matches kept coming and there in the dark suddenly a spark
and god said well I'll be.

Taxes

not only are butterflies free but the citizenry since it stands to
reason graduated self-aggrandizement is good and true because everyone
knows capitalists own big black cars seized by the shortage so that VW
owners everywhere can afford the bowls where the State Marching
Band of America rolls in the new year's hangman on the astroturf gee
this is swell letters whole words out of human beings reading the spirit
of seventy-six mommies and daddies gathered in the name of look at all
that talent crying combine and conquer on the fifty yard line whiskers
peeking out of panties releasing the fiery baton straight up
endoverendoverendoverendover gravity retarding progress climbing near
the peak freeze frame.

Death

what a fan we have in Jesus that he makes it to all the games
yelling your mother was a wishbone at the referees cheering the opposing
teams when finally the officials can take it no longer entering the stands

ripping him link from limb smashing the bones for the marrow though he has left his body behind to terrorize Andre Breton and Salvador Dali whose chocolate chessmen are melting in their hands not in their mouths chanting the janitor is sweeping the bastardly bones like popcorn from the isles while the fan keeps turning despite the ceremony of the unplugging.

Afterlife

where presidents submit voluntarily to polygraphs where there are eight by ten stills of every moment of your life on file where on the great and glorious day you are exposed masturbating before the masses where nightmares are only the beginning where in the end you are found to be a most amazing replica of the replica which is you and now and forever shall be despite your fervent desire to remain anonymous where *where* is a figment of your photographic mind which is your death which is proof enough that after the afterlife there is no life where false advertising got its name where kleenx clouds floating cotton balls pearls pillars and promises of a temperate climate are a euphemism for absolute zero where personalities are so perfect forty-eleven may occupy the point of a pin one point in a locus of nowhere.

Space

some answers don't have questions mouths the drowning fish yanked from the water onto the bank gills going like a throbbing cock praying air air everywhere yet nary a molecule to drink flopping over like a question mark to give it a crack on the other side he hates the land and suffers from fear of phobias which have gathered around the fire singing those old-timey tunes eating their trout and whey when along comes a rider out of the night slashing z's in the seat of their consciousness tiny white bones floating in their bodies entering the blood stream shooting the frothing rapids for the brain.

Time

god is great attendance is good this time of the year and baked ham and candied yams are even greater so that all over America folding chairs are wiped clean arranged to accommodate the many mana from heaven descending upon a plague of come one come all comes the tiger with the lily in his teeth a hollow hungry growl from the storage tanks scribbling on the john walls all the road home for the holidays there is no crisis like ours after such forgiveness what knowledge?

Revelation

An angel lands in Electronics in a nearly deserted discount store.

How sheer the angel—hair, hands, feet, face—as sheer as the gown or even the wings that make it possible the angel should land here!

A child playfully circling a rack of clothes is all who sees, for the clerk occupies the father before a VCR.

A boombox so big no child could lift catches the angel's eye.
Pinpoints of light set deep within the speakers are stars to the angel.
The child knows the angel is looking for a way out.
Mother is in a changing room.
The child has been told to be an angel.
This is funny to the child.
Yet it is the angel who laughs.

Or is it sudden music the child mistakes for laughter, notes so quick and light it is the child who lifts the box by the handle, testing the weight, the music owning affinity with air.

Because the angel.
The angel is flown.

The World Is Ugly and the People Are Sad

The people have done wrong. They have impeached the president. Each night on CNN he enters their homes, pounding a kind of gavel, his fist, from which partially extends a finger. They sit there and they take it. It is the finger the president uses. It is the finger he uses to push their button.

The Finger

The finger squats in the hand, waiting to be said. Longer than other fingers, he is the most difficult to conceal. Blackboard pointer, nose picker . . . we all know when he's here and what he's come for. The finger is not subtle. He knows no rank, no color, no national boundaries. He may be spoken by anyone to anyone: old ladies, young girls. You may even discover yourself producing the finger—a member of the choir, a bank teller, a policeman, or president. The finger knows no occupation except to know them all. Christ himself owned two.

There Was Nobody Famous

There was nobody famous. There were only holes where, on another world, the masses huddled in numbers so large stadiums were built.

All the orchestra wore hoods instead of tuxedos and long dresses. Someone in the audience might cough and a blank program flash and flap like a dove from beneath the robes of a magician.

This means, of course, that the holes were not without substance. As wide as they were deep, we wept for our strangeness.

The They in "What will they think of next?"

They are our real presidents, ruling a kingdom of dumb wonder and vague possibilities. It is an unconscious conspiracy of superior intelligence, of course. The fathers of clever daughters, the mothers of style and invention. We crave what they offer, technologies we eat and excrete, only to find we've been suckling at the cheek of the beautiful dreamchild who crawled in our laps. The baby becomes boy, the boy man. Now we know the future is over in an instant, finite as a cassette in the camera pointed in the wind of time, whirring. There is suspense: how will the past appear? If only there were reason to suspend disbelief. Oppenheimer was one of them. You and I would be but would never fit in. They write, and we *recite* the poem.

Where Silence Rains

Now, as we look upon this child's poster of the biosphere—the moose on Canadian soil staring us in the face, an elephant cake walking the dark continent, the new world monkey hanging by its tail, a lush parrot large enough to serve as the counterpart of a stark polar bear treading from isle to isle, and giraffes peeking over the horizon—how could we not have known Earth is an ark?

Such a thought makes the waters of space more dark as we bob in imagination with nothing here for the light to strike, the whole atmosphere below become an aviary, land a refuge where any winged thing might light.

Tell us, Lord, was *your* list this complete? Did it start with aardvark? We forget the greenhouse. Was there an aquarium for fresh water fish? We picture porpoises off the bow, a whale starboard and another trailing aft, wife and family snug below deck.

For our sake, admit it. Fact is he was crazy. He would've had to have a computer to keep track. And what about species five billion of his offspring haven't found yet? Let's face it. Some of us hear a voice, and on that we act.

Speak then, Lord, of the larger ark, of a promise seemingly as far from honest as fingers crossed behind the back. And if not yours, from whose wrath do we now take flight? From whence will come an olive branch if the voyage ends only where it began?

Faith

A maiden sleepwalking in a field with the moon on her gown, her back toward us—give her the face of whomever, yet remember she is faceless, that were we even to try, our shouts could not name nor awaken her, she for whom memory is mortal, though she is bound to our poems as we are to Earth.

Thus she is the path to Earth, and it is no angel who will pass through her, though lightning be from heaven and white, yet erratic as Mother Nature's quarrels with her spouse. No. But the storm is to be adored as is the moonlight.

If God is the father, he abandons his children. If he is light, he travels so fast we do not see him go by. If, on the other hand, light is seen as metaphor, meaning, literally, radiation, he is everywhere at once. Picture the girl and we picture him. Prayer or poem—God the father or God of light—*faith*, like a blindfold against the night.

Miracle

A man wakes up to find the tattoo on his chest gone. "Jesus," he says, "I don't remember a thing."

This is the syndrome of the state of grace in the state of Wisconsin where, more often than not, a man discovers yet another tattoo *and* the sin of no recollection on his breath.

Later that morning his wife will stare at herself standing by a stranger in her wedding pictures. For she's never known him, this man without his tattoo, the prince lying beside her, and she is suddenly moved to cover herself. Now, with the blanket bunched at her mouth, what might have been a cry is a muffled bellowing.

Because this is Sheboygan, Wisconsin. The man is in a state of grace. And were you able to enter the man's head, you too would know it as a miracle, his condition, the state of having been spared in spite of future transgressions, the moment even before you saw yourself in the mirror, the instant you said to yourself of your wife, "You cow."

The Black Brick

A lady wakes up in a dream in which she's not had a dream in her life. There she lies in an anterior room for a man who induces dreams for a living the way a doctor might induce labor.

What is impossible for her to know is during her preparation she will reveal to the man that while sleeping her brain is like a black brick, is like a thick stanza in a dark poem she tried to write.

The lady drifts off but snaps back. She is paralyzed by two people talking at cross purposes in each of her ears. The one is telling her she is barren, and the woman, her mother, whispers there is no shame in never having had a dream when half of the Earth's inhabitants have never given birth to one but why not find another husband.

Her husband, the person in her other ear, is without sympathy. It is because she will not allow herself to remember her dream, he insists, that his name will not survive. It is because her mother never really wanted her, product she is of another kind of desire.

Of course her husband is right. She will go to her grave without having had a dream in her dream. She will lie in her coffin, feet erect, knees locked, and with folded wings, as if dreaming about being inside a black brick.

Cold Feet

What Adam had said was, "In the time it would take me to warm your feet with mine, I could die of exposure."

Her silence could have been a siren on CNN.

Then they made the kind of love void of clichés.

For the first time in years he awoke sitting on the edge of the bed, a dream so frightening and persistent that to escape it was as much a part of it. He had returned to the town of his birth at the invitation of the university where he would acquire through an enormous salary the home of her dreams. Though wooden, inside the house unfolded into an infinite number of adjoining rooms, each containing different brands of an identical furnishing, so that there was the table room, the chair room, the piano room, the can opener room . The last such space from which he fled contained what he could not remember.

It was a dumb dream.

It had nothing to do with him.

Let alone television or cold feet.

The Tailgater

Adam could count her eyelashes in the rear view mirror, she drove that close. It was as if she needed to know his license plate, myopic and without a memory on her way to work.

Yet her true state was obliviousness. She spent as much time in the mirror as he, touching herself up the last few blocks before they wheeled into the lot.

He'd park in his spot, she in hers, and he'd fumble and dwell for a while as she gathered her keys, her purse, and passed by his rear window for the office, and he'd catch a glimpse of her ass.

What irritated him most was at night on the way home he would have forgotten to adjust his mirror. What irritated her even more was her need to behave as though he wasn't there.

The Betrayal

Adam is home with a little window over his heart he had done at the hospital. Eve thinks it so exotic she begs him to introduce her to the surgeon responsible.

Upon waking in the recovery room, Eve has a headache. Later, Adam races to her beside to find her in a hand mirror, screaming. It seems the window has been implanted in her forehead.

"How could He do this to me?" she cries.

Adam doesn't understand. When finally she sleeps and he quietly reaches over and taps the Plexiglas with his fingernail, microscopic organisms huddle and nudge the other side, as if expecting a handout.

The Loaves and the Fishes

The real mystery is that with an order like that you'd have to phone in ahead. You'd have to say something like, "Yes, for a party of five thousand," and the voice would have to be convincing. Well, you know how that goes. With cynicism running rampant in the world, your story better be good.

For one thing, there are requirements. The loaves must be of a certain size so that your disciple hunkered down in that hollow rock upon which a false-bottomed basket rests has room to maneuver. Perhaps it isn't so preposterous when you consider a gross of a gross of loaves would cut it. Why, there would even be enough for seconds all around and maybe leftovers!

The tricky thing is the fish. In that blazing sun it's got to be a fresh catch. Then there's the problem of distribution, especially with the fish. Do the people form a line? Or do you allow them to circle the mountain, given the distinct possibility that before lunch is over there are those who, fishtails in hand, will be slapping one another as if with rubber chickens.

Logistics. Better to go with canned sardines.

Two Religions

Startled by the flap and gargle of a cock pheasant flushed from the brittle cornstalks along the road you walk beyond the haunt of a sandhill crane, who rose just as it does each morning in slow motion over the curve and mirror of the river, until finally the great bird banks, lands, and gathers wing, a quiet splash that collapses back into itself, Buddhist priest, unlike that Christian clergyman you instantly knew by his collar, who, into the blue, flew.

Testaments

I.

In the end I was as pleased with my performance as a Betty Davis might have been in a picture from a no-name director, God done in the voice of John Houston, before Roman Polanski made his face famous. Even with the script written with me in mind, I declined a nude scene, which nearly killed the story yet somehow preserved the fiction. Friction arose between us—not just Adam but the three of us. Let it be known, though, God had nothing to do with this. I hid because I'm deathly afraid of snakes. The reason you never hear me scream is complicated as the magic of movie making. Let's call it a good editor and a greater soundman. Suffice it to say I never knew what was about to jump out next. I was having trouble concentrating. We moved the whole project off location, which helped me with my character. Adam and I could have retired on our share. Lord knows, a little piece of real estate is all we ever wanted from the beginning. Instead, He handed us the world. As for the snake, he comes and goes as he pleases. The moral of the story is three's a crowd.

II.

Fact is He is. I'm proof enough. Picture pestilence: the picture of blisters and boils. He wrote, produced, and directed it. Break a leg, the company said. He broke my body. On behalf of the entire cast and crew, I thank you for wanting me to give it up. Without you, there would have been no struggle. Yet, the show must go on—that too being part of the storyline. What you wanted me to surrender was faith, all right, but in *life* or, more precisely, my life. What would the Buddha say about that, about his suffering? His brother, Jesus? Sure, I get my reward in the end, though not in heaven, not how I expected but a weeping Robert Duvall playing me leaning on a hoe. What about the beans and berries a giant crushes in order to weed His one thistle, which from the beginning there was little reason to touch, let alone pluck. Maybe greatness is no measure of a man; neither maybe is nobility. How would you know when it's a know-nothing universe, Stanley Kubrick standing there in the abstract. With only the humans in the audience posing questions, the big mystery is both fiction and a fiction.

III.

Like Louise Fletcher's Nurse Ratchet, He was never so happy as when someone was ill. He had the gift to heal, all right. I ought to know. I got well. "Isn't this swell," I say to myself, "four days I'm in heaven, and then it's pure hell." What the gospel doesn't tell is after He had my hands, feet, and face unwrapped, like Boris Karloff or Claude Raines I had to be re-bound. And me then with a price on my head because a few Jews saw and believed! Shouldn't He have—instead of rolled—exploded the stone? Wouldn't others have then seen? After all, how could anyone know I was gone, even though I surely never looked more dead. Nor had been. Why should I now pretend? I'm a high plains drifter, anchor dragging in the sand, pale rider with nothing to avenge. Or the anti-hero, the kid who got away in *Ride the Whirlwind*, the one who by losing won, second banana to Cameron Mitchel—an old version of the young yet uninspired Jack Nicholson.

IV.

In it came on a silver tray, the same design Mother chose for the meal. Ceremoniously the servants set it down. I dared to look right at it; it dared to stare back, such a dreamy look with the room all aghast, subjects seated all on the stone steps. Suddenly I felt like dancing, and the face was Fred Astaire. I lifted it by the hair, swung it here, swung it there, swung it like a dead man swings; then, like a rock caught in a sling, flung it across the banquet hall, blood trailing everywhere, and before it reached the top of its arc, before it headed for my mother's chair, before it landed to lie in her lap like a leopard to its lair, I'd spun thrice in the dead air, debonair as a Cyd Charisse. There. I'd kept her secret. No one had known but the one who couldn't say no to Mother until the deed was done. Like Benjamin and Mrs. Robinson.

V.

Call me Pinocchio. No, on second thought, don't call me—I'll call You, though I'll not beckon like the dead Gregory Peck in *Moby Dick* anymore. Neither will I bleat beneath the skin of a ewe nor even a ram, prototype for Your next sacrificial lamb who in another millennium will suffer a credibility problem in the form of Max Von Sydow, Robert Powell, and Willem Defoe. Mary, Mary, Mary—three drag queens in a row, none sufficiently contrary, man enough for me, in spite of Martin Scorsese. Now don't go getting hysterical again. The echo you hear may be your own, if you truly are our Guardian Angel, my pocket Jimminy Cricket hollering in a hollow whale instead of the cramped entrails of the fish Someone caught using me for bait, a worm powerless to eat its way out, unlike another worm we both know. In the future, why not pick on an actor, someone to play the villain *or* fool? How about Alan Arkin? On second thought, do us all a favor. The next time You want a messenger boy, find a planet where they don't cast lots but plots. The next time you're confused—in the dark, so to speak—make like the blind Audrey Hepburn. Douse the devil in gasoline and dub the scene with the refrain from David Lynch's *Wild at Heart*. Strike a match. And do stand back, Gepetto, old boy.

The Sentence

Yours are the only ears hearing it commuted. The hole in the glass conforms precisely to the shape of your pain plummeting to the courthouse concrete, where a crowd fails to gather the anarchy of your smile, teeth like popcorn for the pigeons on the steps, a certificate in your fist.